Muffins

FAST AND FANTASTIC

THIRD EDITION

SUSAN REIMER

CHERRY TREE PUBLICATIONS
EDINBURGH

Muffins
FAST AND FANTASTIC

Published by Cherry Tree Publications, Edinburgh
Visit www.cherrytreepublications.co.uk

Photography by Richard Mountney, design by Charles Barr

First published in Great Britain 1996
Reprinted 1996, 1997 (four times), 1998 (four times)
Second edition, revised and enlarged 1999
Reprinted 1999 (three times), 2000 (three times)
Third edition, revised and enlarged June 2001
Reprinted November 2001, 2002 (twice), 2003 (twice), 2004, 2006
Revised and reprinted 2008

British Library Cataloguing in Publication Data
Data available

ISBN 978 0 9528858 3 2

(3rd edition: ISBN 0 9528858 2 4)
(2nd edition: ISBN 0 9528858 1 6)
(1st edition: ISBN 0 9528858 0 8)

Printed in Great Britain by Oxuniprint
part of Oxford University Press

CONTENTS

ACKNOWLEDGMENTS

Even a small book can incur many debts of gratitude:
I owe my greatest thanks to my husband for believing in this
"little project" and giving his indefatigable support.

To Richard and Charlie, thank you for making a dream come true!

Useful feedback was provided by the Centre for Nutrition
and Food Research at Queen Margaret College in Edinburgh,
and the Department of Diabetes at the Royal Infirmary in
Edinburgh.

Rombauer and Becker's *Joy of Cooking* was an invaluable
source of information which almost always had answers to my
questions.

I greatly appreciate the bountiful enthusiasm and helpful
comments given by family and friends. This book would not be
the same without them.

Special thanks to my Mum for teaching me the joys of fresh
baking and much more. Your baking was the inspiration for
many of these recipes.

To my wonderful husband, daughter and son

Who, having tested millions of muffins, are happy to eat
millions more.

INTRODUCTION

"What do you call these? Are they cakes? buns? cookies?" When I first published *Muffins* in 1996, muffins were largely unknown in Britain. Now, with the recent explosion of interest in international foods, I am happy to say that those perplexed responses to my Canadian baking are quite rare. In fact, *Muffins* has received an overwhelmingly positive response and as a result has gone through successive editions. For many people, *Muffins* has not only prompted their first attempts at home-baking, but has provided their first successes as well.

Among the enhancements in this third edition, I am pleased to include recipes and tips for delicious gluten-free and wheat-free muffins; this spells the end to dense powdery odd-tasting baking! The information provided will also be helpful for adapting your own recipes to suit gluten- and wheat-free diets.

The muffins in this book are simple to make and quick to bake, as well as being nutritious. This makes them a great alternative to junk food! Crisps and chocolate bars, which dominate today's snack scene, offer little nutritional value: crisps are high in both fat and salt while chocolate bars are high in fat and sugar. Home-made muffins, on the other hand, offer a good balance of carbohydrate, protein and fat. Many of them contain the added goodness of fruits, vegetables, nuts, oats and bran. Muffins are economical to make and offer a wide variety of delicious options: some are traditionally eaten at breakfast, but all are suitable for snacks and tea-time. With flavours covering the whole spectrum of sweet to savoury, there is plenty of choice here for everyone!

The history of the North American muffin is elusive. The flat yeast-leavened "English" muffin bears no resemblance to the peaked cake-like "American" muffin which uses baking powder as its raising agent.

The latter type of muffin can be found in late 19th century American cookery books but its origins and development are difficult to trace. With recipes early travelling north into Canada, the muffin was soon shared between those two cultures. Over the past few decades, muffin popularity has grown to such an extent that they can be commonly found right across Canada and the United States. Muffins are still changing and developing today: trans-Atlantic visitors may have encountered the recent fashion for "mega muffins" and "muffin tops"! Whatever happens with these fads, they bear witness to the infinite adaptability of the muffin.

Muffins were an integral part of my Canadian lifestyle. Baking them each week to enjoy fresh, as well as to stock the freezer for snacks and lunch-boxes, was a basic part of family routine. This came under threat when I first moved to Britain. Anyone who has had opportunity to bake in both Britain and North America will know that some recipes cannot be simply transferred from one country to another. Frustration grows as favourite recipes fail, time after time, for no apparent reason. Eventually my love of baking spurred me on to find the answer.

Two main problems emerged: flour and measurement. The difference in flour accounts for the majority of "flops". You can read more about this under "Notes on Muffin-Making". Likewise the difference in measurement creates no end of trouble. For instance, many people do not realize that a "cup" in North America is a standard measure of 8 fluid ounces (240 ml), whereas a "cup" in Britain can apparently range from 6-10 fluid ounces depending on the size of one's teacup!

Compounding this problem, there is also confusion over the word "ounce". In Canada and the United States, "ounce" is assumed to mean "fluid ounce", as North Americans are accustomed to measuring all ingredients by volume. Indeed, my standard Canadian measuring jug which indicates "ounces" on its side is actually measuring "fluid ounces"; this use of the word "ounce" in North America must not be confused with weight measure. On page 64, I have included approximate volume equivalents for the weights used in this book.

Once the mystery had been unravelled, I began to make muffins again in earnest and was delighted by the interest and enthusiasm shown by friends here. Thus inspired, I set to work developing muffin recipes for the British kitchen, keeping two criteria firmly in mind: they must be nutritious *and* tasty. Over the years, I have encountered many muffin recipes that are no different from cake, and also recipes that try to be so healthy as to be almost inedible! With my background in health sciences, naturally I am keen to promote healthy eating. But with two hungry teenagers, I also know the importance of making food that tastes good! By using low to moderate amounts of sugar and fat, I have tried to achieve a well-balanced muffin.

Every one of these muffins is a favourite in our home and has been tested many, many times. My aim is to give you a delicious and successful introduction to the world of muffins. For most, the variety offered in this book will be more than sufficient for a lifetime of muffin-baking. And for those who have an insatiable appetite for new and different flavours, this book will give the confidence and know-how to develop those individual muffin creations.

The technique for making muffins is simple, but quite different from other forms of baking. So please read the following notes on muffin-making before you begin – following them can make the difference between success and failure! Paragraphs marked by ➤ offer advice for special diets.

Sift together dry ingredients.

Stir together wet ingredients.

Pour wet mixture into dry and stir just to combine. Spoon lumpy batter into muffin tins.

NOTES ON MUFFIN-MAKING

MEASURING AND MIXING

Standardized measuring spoons and jug are essential for successful baking. All measurements with the spoons are level unless stated otherwise. Measurements in the jug should be made at eye-level for accuracy.

Muffin mixing is very quick and simple. In fact, the key to successful muffins is to keep the mixing as brief as possible once the wet and dry ingredients are combined. Generally the dry ingredients are sifted together in one bowl, and the wet ingredients are stirred together in a separate bowl. (The dry ingredients can be prepared in advance but wet and dry must not be combined until just before baking, as liquid will activate the raising agent.) The wet mixture is then poured all at one time into the dry and the two are stirred – not beaten – just until combined. This final mixing must be with a spoon, never a whisk or electric mixer. It should take only about 30 seconds, just until the batter appears evenly mixed but still lumpy. No dry flour should be visible. I prefer to use a metal dessert spoon for stirring as it is more effective than a wooden spoon for scraping the bottom and sides of the bowl during mixing. Muffin batter should not pour ribbon-like off the spoon, but rather should drop in loose globs. I call this a "good dropping consistency" – not too thick, not too thin. Some batters are slightly thicker and drop off the spoon more slowly. I call this a "thick dropping consistency". If your batter is too thick, add a little extra liquid.

Over-stirring has a detrimental effect on the flour which will result in a disappointing muffin. With British plain flour, over-stirring breaks down the delicate gluten, producing a dense texture. In North America, all-purpose flour contains a tougher gluten which produces a coarse texture when over-stirred.

INGREDIENTS

Flour – plain flour, produced from soft wheat, contains a delicate form of gluten which makes it ideal for muffin-making (as with cakes and pastry). Strong flour (for bread-making) on the other hand, is made from hard wheat which contains much more and tougher gluten; this produces an elasticity suitable for yeast-leavened breads but not muffins.

Self-raising flour is an acceptable alternative to plain flour. If this is your flour of choice, note the alterations given for the amount of baking powder required. Do not omit bicarbonate of soda when it is called for. Two notes here: one drawback of self-raising flour is that it is difficult to ensure the raising agent is fresh, especially if you do not bake regularly. Second, self-raising flour in North America usually contains salt; in this case you should omit the salt called for in the recipe. In Britain, self-raising flour does not contain salt.

Wholemeal flour can be used in place of white flour. However I would recommend a half-and-half combination to maintain a light texture. For those who are less keen on wholemeal flour, even substituting a small amount, say 1-2 oz (30-60 g), will increase the fibre and nutritional content.

Two further important points about flour. First, sifting the flour together with the raising agent and salt will ensure an even distribution and minimize lumps. Second, be prepared to adjust the amount of liquid if you are finding the batter too thick or thin. Flour varies in its ability to absorb moisture depending on the type of wheat, processing and storage. Also, after experimenting with several brands of plain flour, I was surprised to find that they produced different volumes for the same weight! All of this made it difficult to give precise liquid measurements. Just bear in mind that most muffin batters should drop off the spoon in loose globs.

In Canada and the United States, all-purpose flour (a blend of soft and hard wheat) is normally used for muffins and breads. When baking in North America, refer to the approximate volume equivalents given on page 64 which can only be a rough guide due to the numerous variables involved. Note that less all-purpose flour is needed than plain flour.

Gluten-free and wheat-free flours are discussed in Appendix 1 (page 60).

Baking powder and **bicarbonate of soda** are not interchangeable. A quick science lesson here: baking powder contains both an acidic and an alkaline substance which react together in the presence of moisture to form a gas; this creates tiny bubbles which expand the batter. Bicarbonate of soda, on the other hand, is solely alkaline. It can only boost the leavening process if used in combination with an acidic ingredient such as yogurt, buttermilk, citrus juice, cocoa or honey. This is usually in addition to the main leavening action carried out by the baking powder. Successful baking is dependent on chemistry: getting the chemistry right not only ensures proper rising but also creates the best flavour, colour and texture. Be sure your raising agents are fresh as their effectiveness deteriorates with time, especially when exposed to air.

Salt is part of the chemistry of baking too and is important for enhancing both texture and flavour. The small amount of salt in these recipes should not be omitted!

Sugar is used both for flavour and texture. Remember that the sugar content of muffins can be adjusted either up or down to suit individual tastes. I have indicated this in a few of the recipes but the same can be done for all. Fine white granulated sugar (such as caster sugar) and soft brown sugars are best as they are easily absorbed into the baked goods. You can substitute one for the other according to preference. White sugar can be mixed with either the wet or dry ingredients, but soft brown sugar distributes better if added to the wet ingredients. Unrefined sugars such as "golden granulated" and "demerara" are not suitable as they will remain gritty in the final product.

➤ *In the diabetic diet it is necessary to restrict sugar intake. A very small amount of sugar in baking is considered acceptable when this is part of an overall healthy diet. The sugar in each of the recipes should be reduced to 2 Tablespoons (30 ml) or less, and sweet toppings, syrups and chocolate should be omitted. It is also important to increase fibre and decrease fat consumed in the diabetic diet. Hence the following recommendations: use a combination of wholemeal and white flour, use reduced fat milk, use vegetable oil rather than butter, and use slightly less oil than stated. Add a little extra liquid to compensate. As the lower sugar and fat content will have an effect on texture, always serve the muffins warm to make this less noticeable.*

Honey is useful not only for its sweetening quality but also its subtle flavour and golden brown colour in baking. When its natural acidity reacts with bicarbonate of soda it can also boost the rising process.

Molasses and **black treacle** can be used interchangeably for the recipes in this book. This is only possible because the stated quantities are small; it does not mean they are the same. Molasses is available in three forms: light table molasses (commonly used in North America), dark molasses, and bitter blackstrap molasses. Black treacle is a blend of dark molasses and other syrups. Take note: when using North American recipes that call for table molasses, substituting black treacle will give disappointing results. Adjustments must be made for black treacle's strong flavour and less acidic properties.

Eggs enhance the texture, rising and nutritional value of baked foods. These recipes are based on medium (size 3 and 4) eggs but other sizes should not be a problem for single batches.

➢ *For those who cannot include eggs in their diet, omit the egg and increase the amount of liquid by 3-4 Tablespoons (45-60 ml). If only the yolk needs to be omitted, substitute 1 or 2 egg whites instead.*

Milk – semi-skimmed, skimmed and whole milk all work equally well. Powdered milk is a very economical alternative to fresh milk, with no noticeable difference in flavour when used in baking.

➢ *For those who cannot include dairy milk in their diet, soya milk is a good alternative. Likewise soya yogurt can be substituted for dairy yogurt.*

Oil – I have specified vegetable oil as it has a mild flavour suitable for baking and usually contains a high proportion of rapeseed oil. Rapeseed oil (also known as canola oil) has become popular recently due to its low saturated fat content and other health benefits. Sunflower oil and corn oil work equally well, but olive oil is not recommended for muffin baking because of its strong flavour.

➢ *You might not be accustomed to using vegetable oil in baking. Dieticians recommend it as a healthier option than butter as it is significantly lower in saturated fat. For many muffin recipes oil gives the best result for texture and flavour as well as being more economical and easier to use. However some recipes require butter for either its flavour or the method of mixing.*

For those who prefer to cut back on the fat content, the quantity can be reduced by 1 fluid ounce (30 ml) vegetable oil or 1 ounce (30 g) butter. The muffins will not be as tender as a result but this can be made less noticeable by serving warm. I do not recommend cutting back any further than this as the texture becomes chewy rather than tender.

Butter – where butter is called for, a suitable margarine can also be used. For health reasons, avoid hard margarines: these contain transfatty acids which apparently do us more harm than saturated fat. (Note: hot melted butter must not be added directly to the beaten egg as it would cook the egg instantly. Always cool the butter slightly and add ingredients in the order given.)

Wheatgerm forms the most nutritious part of the wheat kernel, and is a natural source of folic acid, vitamin E, thiamine and iron. It has a mild nutty flavour, and should be stored in the refrigerator. A spoonful of wheatgerm can be added to all your baking for extra nutrition.

Fruit – dried fruit tends to absorb moisture from the batter, whereas fresh fruit and vegetables release juice into the batter during baking. This should be kept in mind when adapting or creating muffin recipes.

BAKING

For best results use proper muffin tins of either standard or mini-size. A standard muffin cup is about 3 cm deep and 7 cm in diameter across the top. Mini-muffins are fun for parties and smaller appetites. The recipes in this book will produce 10-12 standard-size muffins or approximately 36 mini-muffins (or 6 standard plus 12 mini!). Extra-large ("Texas-style") tins will enable you to make 5 or 6 jumbo muffins.

Shallow bun tins are not recommended, as the muffins cannot achieve their correct shape and height. However, if this is all that is available, decrease baking time to about 15 minutes.

Prepare your muffin tins either by lining with paper cases or by greasing with a solid vegetable fat or margarine. Oil sprays are also available in most supermarkets. If using grease, allow muffins to cool for several minutes to make removal easier. Cooling also helps paper cases peel off more easily.

Ideally, muffins have a raised symmetrical top although the actual height will depend on the contents of the batter and how much is put into each muffin cup. Several factors can prevent a muffin from rising properly: low oven temperature, stale raising agent, overly thick batter (muffins are hard and small) or thin batter (muffins spread out over the pan instead of up). Very pointy or distorted tops indicate the oven temperature is too hot or uneven.

Muffins should be baked in a moderately hot, preheated oven, so 375-400°F (190-200°C) in a conventional oven. For fan ovens, the temperature should be lowered to approximately 170°C (refer to the manufacturer's instructions). With a gas oven, use Gas Mark 5-6 if baking on the middle rack, or Gas Mark 4-5 if baking nearer the top of the oven. Ovens vary in their temperature distribution and accuracy so you will need to discover what works best with yours.

Standard-size muffins should take about 20-25 minutes to bake in a conventional or gas oven, mini-muffins about 15 minutes and jumbo muffins about 30-35 minutes. Muffins are done when the tops are lightly browned and spring back (or feel quite firm) when pressed gently. If your finger leaves an indent, continue baking for another 2-3 minutes and test again. (For jumbo muffins, it is best to test with a metal cake-tester as the top can become brown before the inside is fully baked.) If the muffins require either more or less time than stated above, make appropriate adjustments to your oven temperature for future batches.

STORING AND FREEZING

Muffins are at their best when freshly baked and still warm. Ideally, any not eaten on the day of baking should be frozen as soon as possible to maintain freshness. Muffins freeze very well. Simply cool them to room temperature and freeze in airtight bags or containers – perfect for taking out whenever needed, and in just the right quantity! If freezing is not possible, store muffins in an airtight container and eat within two days. Warm before serving to restore freshness.

A frozen muffin, wrapped in a lunch box first thing in the morning, will be thawed by lunch-time. For instant thawing, microwave unwrapped at Medium for 30-40 seconds. With a conventional oven, heat frozen muffins for 10-15 minutes at 350°F (175°C), unwrapped for a crusty muffin, wrapped in foil for a soft one.

THE BASIC MUFFIN

The basic muffin invites creative variation! Try different combinations of dried fruit, berries, nuts and chocolate chips, or simply enjoy the plain muffin fresh from the oven with your favourite jam. Since the sugar and fat content is lower than cake, muffins are best served fresh and warm – uneaten muffins should be frozen on the same day if possible. In this version of the basic muffin the natural acidity of yogurt reacts with soda bicarbonate to produce a light texture. As with all muffin recipes, the sugar can be adjusted to suit your taste. For best results, please read the essential muffin-making tips on pages 7-10 before you begin.

Makes 10-11 standard-size

10 oz (280 g) plain flour*
2 teaspoons (10 ml) baking powder
$^1/_2$ teaspoon (2.5 ml) bicarbonate of soda
$^1/_4$ teaspoon (1.2 ml) salt
1 egg
3-5 oz (85-140 g) fine white granulated sugar or light brown
    soft sugar
4 fl oz (120 ml) plain yogurt
5 fl oz (150 ml) milk (adjust if necessary to give a good
    dropping consistency – not too thick, not too thin)
3 fl oz (90 ml) vegetable oil
1 teaspoon (5 ml) vanilla essence (optional)

With self-raising flour, omit baking powder; do not omit bicarbonate of soda.

Method

1 Prepare muffin tins with liners or grease. Preheat oven to 375-400°F (190-200°C) for a conventional oven, Gas Mark 5-6. (See page 10 for fan ovens and further guidelines.)

2 In a large bowl, sift together flour, baking powder, bicarbonate of soda and salt.

3 In a separate bowl, beat egg with a fork. Stir in sugar, yogurt, milk, oil and vanilla.

4 Scrape all of liquid mixture into dry. Using a metal spoon, stir lightly until evenly combined, scraping the sides and bottom of the bowl as you stir. This mixing should take only about 30 seconds. The batter should have a good dropping consistency. Ignore the lumpy appearance of the batter.

5 Fill muffin cups three-quarters full. Bake about 20 minutes until tops are lightly browned and spring back when pressed gently.

Berry Muffins

Add 4 oz (110 g) berries, folding them into the final batter. Chop large berries. Do not thaw frozen berries; bake an extra 3-4 minutes. (For other berry muffins, see pages 20, 36, 44, 50 and 58.)

Chocolate Chip Muffins

Add 3 oz (85 g) plain chocolate chips.

Dried Fruit Muffins

Many varieties of dried fruit are now available such as cranberry and tropical fruit. Use about 4 oz (110 g).

Note: For a milk-only version of the Basic Muffin, use 3 teaspoons (15 ml) baking powder and 8 fl oz (240 ml) milk; omit soda bicarbonate and yogurt. If using self-raising flour for this version, reduce baking powder to 1 teaspoon (5 ml).

Photo opposite: chocolate chip mini-muffins

APPLE SPICE MUFFINS

Always a popular flavour! Adjust the sugar and spice to suit your taste. Mixed spice (not to be confused with allspice) is a lovely blend of sweet spices including cinnamon, coriander seed, caraway seed, nutmeg, ginger and cloves.

Makes 11-12 standard-size

9 oz (255 g) plain flour*
3 teaspoons (15 ml) baking powder
$^1/_4$ teaspoon (1.2 ml) salt
1$^1/_2$ teaspoons (7.5 ml) mixed spice (or try 1$^1/_2$ teaspoons cinnamon plus $^1/_4$ teaspoon nutmeg and a pinch of ginger and cloves)
1 egg
4 oz (110 g) fine white granulated sugar
6 oz (170 g) finely chopped apple (I like to use Granny Smiths, but most other types should work just as well)
5 fl oz (150 ml) milk (adjust if necessary to give a thick dropping consistency)
3 fl oz (90 ml) vegetable oil
2-3 oz (60-85 g) raisins, sultanas or chopped walnuts (optional)

Optional Topping:
3 Tablespoons (45 ml) soft brown sugar
2 oz (60 g) walnuts, chopped

*With self-raising flour, reduce baking powder to 1 teaspoon (5 ml).

Method

1 Prepare muffin tins. Preheat oven to 375-400°F (190-200°C) for a conventional oven, Gas Mark 5-6.

2 In a large bowl, sift together flour, baking powder, salt and spice.

3 In another bowl, beat egg with a fork. Stir in sugar, chopped apple, milk and oil.

4 Pour all of wet mixture into dry. Stir lightly until combined and no dry flour is visible. Add dried fruit/walnuts during the final strokes. This batter should have a thick dropping consistency; apple releases juice as it cooks.

5 Spoon into tins. Sprinkle with topping. Bake about 20-25 minutes until tops are lightly browned and spring back when pressed gently. Cool for several minutes to make removal easier.

APRICOT ALMOND MUFFINS

Toasted almonds and apricots make a delicious combination while the natural acidity of yogurt enhances the texture and flavour. You can use either plain or apricot yogurt.

Makes 12 standard-size

2 oz (60 g) toasted flaked almonds (instructions given below)
10 oz (280 g) plain flour*
2 teaspoons (10 ml) baking powder
1/2 teaspoon (2.5 ml) bicarbonate of soda
1/4 teaspoon (1.2 ml) salt
1 egg
4-5 oz (110-140 g) fine white granulated sugar or light brown soft sugar
1 teaspoon (5 ml) vanilla essence
6 oz (170 g) dried apricots, chopped
6 fl oz (180 ml) milk
4 fl oz (120 ml) plain or apricot yogurt
3 fl oz (90 ml) vegetable oil

Method

1 Prepare muffin tins. Preheat oven to 375-400°F (190-200°C) for a conventional oven, Gas Mark 5-6.
2 To toast flaked almonds: spread on a baking sheet and bake for about 5 minutes until lightly browned.
3 In a large bowl, sift together flour, baking powder, bicarbonate of soda and salt.
4 In another bowl, beat egg with a fork. Stir in sugar, vanilla, apricots, milk, yogurt, oil and almonds.
5 Scrape all of wet mixture into dry. Stir lightly just until evenly combined and no dry flour is visible.
6 Fill muffin cups three-quarters full. Bake for about 20 minutes until tops are lightly browned and spring back when pressed gently.

With self-raising flour, omit baking powder; do not adjust bicarbonate of soda.

BANANA MUFFINS

A perennial favourite that never fails to please! It might help to know that ripe bananas can be frozen in an airtight container, ready to be used at your convenience.

Makes 11-12 standard-size

10 oz (280 g) plain flour*
1 teaspoon (5 ml) baking powder
1 teaspoon (5 ml) bicarbonate of soda
1/4 teaspoon (1.2 ml) salt
8-10 fl oz (240-290 ml) ripe banana purée (about 3 medium bananas)
4 oz (110 g) fine white granulated sugar
1 egg, beaten with a fork
3 fl oz (90 ml) milk or water
3 fl oz (90 ml) vegetable oil
2-3 oz (60-85 g) walnuts or plain chocolate chips (optional)

Method

1 Prepare muffin tins. Preheat oven to 375-400°F (190-200°C) for a conventional oven, Gas Mark 5-6.
2 In a large bowl, sift together flour, baking powder, bicarbonate of soda and salt. (Add chocolate if using.)
3 In another bowl, mash bananas thoroughly with a potato masher until puréed. Stir in sugar, egg, milk/water and oil. (Add walnuts or oats if using.)
4 Pour all of wet mixture into dry. Stir just until batter is evenly mixed but still lumpy. No dry flour should be visible.
5 Spoon into tins. Bake about 20 minutes until tops are lightly browned and spring back when pressed gently.

With self-raising flour, omit baking powder; do not alter bicarbonate of soda.

Banana Oatmeal Muffins
Reduce flour to 8 oz (225 g). Add 2 oz (60 g) rolled oats and 1-2 tablespoons extra liquid.

BRAN MUFFINS

Cultured buttermilk is a low-fat product that gives a special flavour and tenderness in baking. These are full of fibre and a pleasure to eat.

Makes 12 standard-size

8 oz (225 g) plain flour*
2 teaspoons (10 ml) baking powder
1 teaspoon (5 ml) bicarbonate of soda
1/4 teaspoon (1.2 ml) salt
1 egg
4-5 oz (110-140 g) light brown soft sugar
2 Tablespoons (30 ml) black treacle, liquid honey or molasses
8 fl oz (240 ml) cultured buttermilk
2 oz (60 g) natural wheat bran
2-3 fl oz (60-90 ml) milk
3 fl oz (90 ml) vegetable oil
3 oz (85 g) raisins, sultanas or chopped dates

Method

1 Prepare muffin tins. Preheat oven to 375-400°F (190-200°C) for a conventional oven, Gas Mark 5-6.
2 In a large bowl, sift together flour, baking powder, bicarbonate of soda and salt.
3 In a medium-sized bowl, beat egg with a fork. Stir in sugar, treacle/honey/molasses, buttermilk, bran, milk and oil.
4 Pour all of wet mixture into dry. Stir lightly just until evenly combined and no dry flour is visible. Add dried fruit during the final strokes.
5 Spoon into tins. Bake about 20 minutes until tops spring back when pressed gently. Best served warm, with or without butter.

With self-raising flour, omit baking powder; do not alter bicarbonate of soda.

Note: To substitute regular milk for buttermilk, omit soda bicarbonate and use 3 teaspoons (15 ml) baking powder. Omit the extra 3 fl oz milk but be prepared to adjust the batter to a good dropping consistency.

BRAN CINNAMON MUFFINS

Here's another delicious way to get bran into your diet.

Makes 10-11 standard-size

3 oz (85 g) bran cereal sticks
10 fl oz (290 ml) milk
7 oz (200 g) plain flour*
3 teaspoons (15 ml) baking powder
1/4 teaspoon (1.2 ml) salt
1 egg, beaten with a fork
3 oz (85 g) light brown soft sugar
3 fl oz (90 ml) vegetable oil

Filling:
2 oz (60 g) light brown soft sugar
2 teaspoons (10 ml) ground cinnamon
3 oz (85 g) sultanas or raisins

Method

1 Prepare muffin tins. Preheat oven to 375-400°F (190-200°C) for a conventional oven, Gas Mark 5-6.
2 In a medium-sized bowl, combine bran cereal sticks and milk. Set aside to soak while you prepare the other ingredients.
3 In a small bowl, stir together filling ingredients and set aside. In a large bowl, sift together flour, baking powder and salt.
4 Now to the bran mixture add beaten egg, sugar and oil.
5 Pour all of wet mixture into dry. Stir just until evenly mixed but still lumpy.
6 Using about half the batter, spoon a small amount into each prepared cup. Cover with filling, and finish with remaining batter. Bake for about 20 minutes, until tops spring back when pressed gently.

With self-raising flour, reduce baking powder to 1 teaspoon (5 ml).

BUTTERMILK MUFFINS

Although its name might suggest otherwise, cultured buttermilk is a low-fat product and its natural acidity reacts with soda bicarbonate to produce a light texture. These are delicious served warm with jam, or alternatively try baking them with the jam already inside as I did for the photo.

Makes 11 standard-size

10 oz (280 g) plain flour*
1½ teaspoons (7.5 ml) baking powder
1 teaspoon (5 ml) bicarbonate of soda
¼ teaspoon (1.2 ml) salt
1 egg
3-4 oz (85-110 g) fine white granulated sugar
8 fl oz (240 ml) cultured buttermilk
3 fl oz (90 ml) milk
3 fl oz (90 ml) vegetable oil

Method

1 Prepare muffin tins. Preheat oven to 375-400°F (190-200°C) for a conventional oven, Gas Mark 5-6.
2 In a large bowl, sift together flour, baking powder, bicarbonate of soda and salt.
3 In a separate bowl, beat egg with a fork. Stir in sugar, buttermilk, milk and oil.
4 Pour all of wet mixture into dry and stir just until combined. Batter will be lumpy but no dry flour should be visible.
5 Spoon immediately into tins, filling three-quarters full. Bake for about 20 minutes until tops are lightly browned and spring back when pressed gently.

With self-raising flour, omit baking powder; do not alter bicarbonate of soda.

Buttermilk Berry Muffins
Add 4 oz (110 g) berries, folding them gently into the final batter. Large berries should be chopped. Do not thaw frozen berries; bake for an extra 3-4 minutes instead.

BUTTERSCOTCH RAISIN MUFFINS

Full of flavour and crunch. A real treat! As with any muffin, adjust the sugar to suit your taste.

Makes 11 standard-size

9 oz (255 g) plain flour*
2 teaspoons (10 ml) baking powder
½ teaspoon (2.5 ml) bicarbonate of soda
¼ teaspoon (1.2 ml) salt
1 egg
3-5 oz (85-140 g) soft brown or fine white granulated sugar
8 fl oz (240 ml) milk
2 teaspoons (10 ml) vanilla essence
3 oz (85 g) butter, melted
4-5 oz (110-140 g) raisins or sultanas
2 oz (60 g) walnuts or pecans, chopped
Golden syrup, maple syrup or North American "corn syrup" for optional topping

Method

1 Prepare muffin tins. Preheat oven to 375-400°F (190-200°C) for a conventional oven, Gas Mark 5-6.
2 In a large bowl, sift together flour, baking powder, bicarbonate of soda and salt.
3 In another bowl, beat egg with a fork. Add sugar, milk and vanilla, followed by melted butter.
4 Pour all of wet mixture into dry. Stir just until combined and no dry flour is visible. Add raisins and nuts during the final strokes.
5 Fill muffin cups three-quarters full. Bake about 20 minutes until tops are lightly browned and feel quite firm. Spread a small spoonful of syrup over each muffin top if desired.

If using self-raising flour, omit baking powder; do not adjust bicarbonate of soda.

CARROT MUFFINS

So moist and delicious, and they don't taste at all like carrots!
These have much less sugar and oil than traditional carrot cake.
The icing is optional, of course.

Makes 11-12 standard-size

10 oz (280 g) plain flour*
2 teaspoons (10 ml) baking powder
1 teaspoon (5 ml) bicarbonate of soda
1/4 teaspoon (1.2 ml) salt
2 teaspoons (10 ml) ground cinnamon
1 egg
4-5 oz (110-140 g) fine white granulated sugar or light
   brown soft sugar
10 oz (280 g) carrot, finely grated or finely chopped in a
   food processor – yields 14 fl oz (400 ml)
1 teaspoon (5 ml) vanilla essence
2 Tablespoons (30 ml) liquid honey
3 fl oz (90 ml) milk or water
3 fl oz (90 ml) vegetable oil
2 oz (60 g) chopped walnuts or raisins (optional)

Icing (traditional with carrot cake):
2 oz (60 g) cream cheese, softened (at room temperature)
4 oz (110 g) icing sugar, sifted
1/4 teaspoon (1.2 ml) vanilla essence

With self-raising flour, omit baking powder; do not adjust bicarbonate of soda.

Method

1 Prepare muffin tins. Preheat oven to 375-400°F
(190-200°C) for a conventional oven, Gas Mark 5-6.
2 In a large bowl, sift together flour, baking powder,
bicarbonate of soda, salt and cinnamon. (Stir in bran if
using.)
3 In a separate bowl, beat egg with a fork. Add sugar, carrot,
vanilla, honey, milk/water and oil. Stir well.
4 Scrape all of liquid mixture into dry. Stir lightly until evenly
combined. (Add walnuts or raisins during the final strokes if
using.) Batter should have a thick dropping consistency;
carrot releases liquid into the batter as it cooks.
5 Spoon into tins. Bake for about 20 minutes until tops spring
back when pressed gently. Allow muffins to cool before
icing. Stir icing ingredients together until blended; thin with
a few drops of water if needed.

Carrot Bran Muffins
Decrease flour to 9 oz (255 g); add 1 oz (30 g) wheat bran to
the dry ingredients.

CHERRY WALNUT MUFFINS

Black, red or glacé cherries will each give a distinct taste and appearance, complemented by the flavour of almond and the crunch of walnuts. Tinned cherries work fine; drain well before using. As with all muffins, adjust the sugar to suit your taste.

Makes 11 standard-size

10 oz (280 g) plain flour*
2 teaspoons (10 ml) baking powder
$^1/_2$ teaspoon (2.5 ml) bicarbonate of soda
$^1/_4$ teaspoon (1.2 ml) salt
1 egg
4 oz (110 g) fine white granulated sugar
4 fl oz (120 ml) plain yogurt
5 fl oz (150 ml) milk
$^1/_2$ teaspoon (2.5 ml) almond essence
3 fl oz (90 ml) vegetable oil
5 oz (140 g) chopped and pitted black or red cherries, or glacé cherries
2 oz (60 g) chopped walnuts

Method

1 Prepare muffin tins. Preheat oven to 375-400°F (190-200°C) for a conventional oven, Gas Mark 5-6.
2 In a large bowl, sift together flour, baking powder, bicarbonate of soda and salt.
3 In a separate bowl, beat egg with a fork. Stir in sugar, yogurt, milk, almond essence and oil.
4 When the oven is ready, pour all of liquid mixture into dry. Stir lightly until combined and no dry flour is visible. Gently fold in cherries and walnuts. The batter should have a thick dropping consistency.
5 Fill muffin cups three-quarters full. Bake for about 20 minutes until tops are lightly browned and spring back when pressed gently.

With self-raising flour, omit baking powder; do not omit soda bicarbonate.

CARROT PINEAPPLE MUFFINS

These are moist and scrumptious. Vary the flavour by including one or more of the optional additions.

Makes 11-12 standard-size

6 oz (170 g) carrot, finely grated or finely chopped by food processor – yields 8 fl oz (240 ml)
4 slices pineapple, finely chopped – yields 4 fl oz (120 ml)
9 oz (255 g) plain flour*
2 teaspoons (10 ml) baking powder
1 teaspoon (5 ml) bicarbonate of soda
$^1/_4$ teaspoon (1.2 ml) salt
2 teaspoons (10 ml) ground cinnamon
1 egg
4 oz (110 g) fine white granulated sugar
3 fl oz (90 ml) milk (or juice from the tinned pineapple)
3 fl oz (90 ml) vegetable oil

Optional Additions:
2 oz (60 g) chopped nuts or raisins
2 Tablespoons (30 ml) desiccated coconut

Method

1 Prepare muffin tins. Preheat oven to 375-400°F (190-200°C) for a conventional oven, Gas Mark 5-6.
2 Prepare carrot and pineapple. Set aside.
3 In a large bowl, sift together flour, baking powder, bicarbonate of soda, salt and cinnamon.
4 In a medium-sized bowl, beat egg with a fork. Add sugar, milk/juice, oil, carrot and pineapple.
5 Scrape all of wet mixture into dry. Stir just until evenly combined and no dry flour is visible. (Add optional ingredients during the final strokes.)
6 Spoon into tins. Bake for 20-25 minutes until tops feel quite firm. (Spread cooled muffins with cream cheese icing, page 22, if desired.)

With self-raising flour omit baking powder; do not omit bicarbonate of soda.

CHOCOLATE MUFFINS

Always a hit! The addition of yogurt makes these especially light and moist. As with any muffin, adjust the sugar to suit your taste.

Makes 12 standard-size

9 oz (255 g) plain flour*
2 teaspoons (10 ml) baking powder
1/2 teaspoon (2.5 ml) bicarbonate of soda
1/4 teaspoon (1.2 ml) salt
1 egg
6 oz (170 g) fine white granulated sugar
1 teaspoon (5 ml) vanilla essence
3 fl oz (90 ml) vegetable oil
4 Tablespoons (60 ml) unsweetened cocoa powder
4 fl oz (120 ml) plain yogurt
5 fl oz (150 ml) milk

Optional toppings: chocolate chips, nuts, desiccated coconut

Method

1 Prepare muffin tins. Preheat oven to 375-400°F (190-200°C) for a conventional oven, Gas Mark 5-6.
2 In a large bowl, sift together flour, baking powder, bicarbonate of soda and salt.
3 In a medium-sized bowl, beat egg with a fork. Add in the order given, combining well after each addition: sugar, vanilla, oil, cocoa powder, yogurt and milk.
4 Pour wet mixture into dry. Stir lightly until evenly combined and no dry flour is visible. Batter should have a good dropping consistency, slightly more loose than others, and with small lumps. (Add any extra bits during the final stirring if using.)
5 Fill muffin cups three-quarters full. (Add topping if using.) Bake about 20 minutes until tops spring back when pressed gently.

With self-raising flour omit baking powder; do not adjust bicarbonate of soda.

CHOCOLATE MUFFIN VARIATIONS

Double Chocolate Muffins
Add 3 oz (85 g) plain chocolate chips.

Chocolate Cheesecake Muffins
Stir together 4 oz (110 g) softened cream cheese and 3 Tablespoons (45 ml) caster (fine granulated) sugar; set aside. Prepare chocolate batter. Using about half the batter, spoon a small amount into each muffin cup. Drop about a teaspoon of cream cheese filling on top, and then finish with remaining chocolate batter. Bake as usual.

Chocolate Cherry Muffins
Add 5 oz (140 g) black cherries, chopped and pitted.

Chocolate Mocha Muffins
Replace milk with 5 fl oz (150 ml) strong coffee: dissolve 3 teaspoons (15 ml) instant coffee granules in 5 fl oz (150 ml) boiling water; cool before using. This recipe can be used in combination with any of the other variations.

Chocolate Nut Muffins
Add 2 oz (60 g) chopped pecans, walnuts, hazelnuts or Brazil nuts to the batter. Nuts can also be used in combination with the other variations of course.

Chocolate Muffins with a Quick Icing
Combine the following icing ingredients, stirring till smooth after each addition:
1 Tablespoon (15 ml) hot melted butter
1 Tablespoon (15 ml) unsweetened cocoa powder
1 Tablespoon (15 ml) hot water
4 oz (110 g) icing sugar, sifted
1/2 teaspoon (2.5 ml) vanilla essence
This icing thickens as it cools. Thin with a few drops of water if needed.

Note: For a milk-only version of the Chocolate Muffin, omit yogurt and increase milk to about 8 fl oz (240 ml). Do not omit soda bicarbonate as it is needed to neutralise the natural acidity of cocoa.

CINNAMON CRUNCH MUFFINS

Layering the batter with a mixture of cinnamon, nuts and sugar gives that extra-special look and taste.

Makes 12 standard-size

10 oz (280 g) plain flour*
2¹/₂ teaspoons (12.5 ml) baking powder
¹/₂ teaspoon (2.5 ml) bicarbonate of soda
¹/₄ teaspoon (1.2 ml) salt
1 egg
2 oz (60 g) fine white granulated sugar
5 fl oz (150 ml) cultured sour cream
6 fl oz (180 ml) milk
2 fl oz (60 ml) vegetable oil
1 teaspoon (5 ml) vanilla essence

For Filling and Topping:
3 oz (85 g) light brown soft sugar
3 oz (85 g) pecans or walnuts, chopped
2 teaspoons (10 ml) ground cinnamon

*With self-raising flour omit baking powder; do not omit bicarbonate of soda.

Method

1 Prepare muffin tins. Preheat oven to 375-400°F (190-200°C) for a conventional oven, Gas Mark 5-6.
2 Combine filling ingredients and set aside.
3 In a large bowl, sift together flour, baking powder, bicarbonate of soda and salt.
4 In a separate bowl, beat egg with a fork. Stir in sugar, sour cream, milk, oil and vanilla.
5 Pour all of liquid mixture into dry. Stir lightly just until evenly combined and no dry flour is visible. Batter should have a good dropping consistency and will appear lumpy.
6 Using approximately half the batter, spoon a small amount into each cup. Sprinkle with half the cinnamon mixture. Spoon out remaining batter and finish with topping. Bake for about 20 minutes until tops spring back when pressed gently.

COCOA COURGETTE MUFFINS

Don't let the name put you off! As with carrot muffins, the courgette ("zucchini" in North America) simply adds moisture and vitamins.

Makes 12 standard-size

10 oz (280 g) plain flour*
2 teaspoons (10 ml) baking powder
1/2 teaspoon (2.5 ml) bicarbonate of soda
1/4 teaspoon (1.2 ml) salt
2 teaspoons (10 ml) ground cinnamon
1 egg
5 oz (140 g) light brown soft sugar
3 fl oz (90 ml) vegetable oil
3 Tablespoons (45 ml) unsweetened cocoa powder
2 teaspoons (10 ml) vanilla essence
12 oz (340 g) courgette, finely grated or finely chopped in a food processor, which will yield about 14 fl oz (400 ml) – no need to peel the courgette, unless you want to avoid green flecks in the finished muffin
2 fl oz (60 ml) milk or water
3 oz (85 g) raisins or sultanas (optional)

Method

1 Prepare muffin tins. Preheat oven to 375-400°F (190-200°C) for a conventional oven, Gas Mark 5-6.
2 In a large bowl, sift together flour, baking powder, bicarbonate of soda, salt and cinnamon.
3 In a medium-sized bowl, beat egg with a fork. Add and stir after each addition: sugar, oil, cocoa powder, vanilla, courgette and milk/water.
4 Scrape all of wet mixture into dry. Stir just until evenly combined, adding dried fruit during the final strokes. Batter should have a thick dropping consistency.
5 Spoon into tins. Bake for about 20 minutes until tops spring back when pressed gently.

If using self-raising flour, omit baking powder; do not adjust bicarbonate of soda.

CORNMEAL MUFFINS

This muffin can work as a savoury or sweet: serve with or without butter to accompany a light meal such as soup, or serve with maple syrup to make a tasty dessert. As with all muffins, adjust the sugar to suit your taste.

Makes 10 standard-size

6 oz (170 g) plain flour*
2 teaspoons (10 ml) baking powder
1/2 teaspoon (2.5 ml) bicarbonate of soda
1/4 teaspoon (1.2 ml) salt
6 oz (170 g) yellow cornmeal
1 egg
2-3 oz (60-85 g) fine white granulated sugar
4 fl oz (120 ml) plain yogurt
6 fl oz (180 ml) milk
3 oz (85 g) butter or margarine, melted

Method

1 Prepare muffin tins. Preheat oven to 375-400°F (190-200°C) for a conventional oven, Gas Mark 5-6.
2 In a large bowl, sift together flour, baking powder, bicarbonate of soda, salt and cornmeal.
3 In another bowl, beat egg with a fork. Stir in sugar, yogurt, milk and melted butter.
4 Scrape all of wet mixture into dry. Stir lightly just until evenly combined. Ignore lumps.
5 Fill muffin cups three-quarters full. Bake for about 20 minutes until edges appear golden brown and tops feel quite firm. Best served warm, with or without butter.

Note: For a milk-only version, omit yogurt and soda bicarbonate; use 3 teaspoons (15 ml) baking powder and about 9 fl oz (260 ml) milk.

CRANBERRY MUFFINS

A tasty muffin, using ready-made cranberry sauce with whole berries. The natural acidity of the yogurt and citrus juice reacts with soda bicarbonate to produce a light texture. To use fresh cranberries, see pages 12, 20, 36, 44 and 58.

Makes 11 standard-size

10 oz (280 g) plain flour*
2 teaspoons (10 ml) baking powder
1/2 teaspoon (2.5 ml) bicarbonate of soda
1/4 teaspoon (1.2 ml) salt
1 egg
4 oz (110 g) fine white granulated sugar
6 fl oz (180 ml) whole-berry cranberry sauce
Finely grated rind of half an orange or lemon – avoid grating
    into the white pith which is bitter
2 Tablespoons (30 ml) fresh orange juice or 1 Tablespoon
    (15 ml) fresh lemon juice
3 fl oz (90 ml) vegetable oil
4 fl oz (120 ml) plain yogurt
3 fl oz (90 ml) milk
2 oz (60 g) chopped pecans or walnuts (optional)

Method

1 Prepare muffin tins. Preheat oven to 375-400°F
(190-200°C) for a conventional oven, Gas Mark 5-6.
2 In a large bowl, sift together flour, baking powder, bicarbonate of
soda and salt.
3 In a separate bowl, beat egg with a fork. Stir in sugar, cranberry
sauce, grated orange or lemon rind, juice, oil, yogurt and milk.
4 When the oven is ready, scrape all of liquid mixture into dry.
Stir lightly until evenly combined. (Add nuts during the final
strokes if using.) Batter should have a thick dropping
consistency.
5 Fill muffin cups three-quarters full. Bake for about 20 minutes
until tops are browned and spring back when pressed gently.

With self-raising flour, omit baking powder; do not omit soda bicarbonate.

DATE WALNUT MUFFINS

A classic combination and an excellent muffin.

Makes 12 standard-size

10 fl oz (290 ml) boiling water
6 oz (170 g) dried stoned dates, chopped
10 oz (280 g) plain flour*
2 teaspoons (10 ml) baking powder
1/2 teaspoon (2.5 ml) bicarbonate of soda
1/4 teaspoon (1.2 ml) salt
1 egg
4 oz (110 g) light brown soft sugar
1 teaspoon (5 ml) vanilla essence
2 oz (85 g) walnuts, chopped
3 oz (85 g) butter, melted

Optional topping: 2 oz (60 g) brown sugar mixed with
    1/2 teaspoon (2.5 ml) cinnamon

Method

1 Pour measured hot water over chopped dates. Set aside to
soak and cool for about 20 minutes. Do not discard water.
2 Prepare muffin tins. Preheat oven to 375-400°F (190-200°C)
for a conventional oven, Gas Mark 5-6.
3 In a large bowl, sift together flour, baking powder, bicarbonate
of soda and salt.
4 In a separate bowl, beat egg with a fork. Stir in sugar, vanilla,
cooled dates and water, walnuts and butter.
5 Pour all of liquid mixture into dry. Stir lightly just until
combined and no dry flour is visible.
6 Fill muffin cups three-quarters full. (Sprinkle with topping if
using.) Bake about 20 minutes until tops spring back when
pressed gently.

With self-raising flour, omit baking powder; do not adjust bicarbonate of soda.

Coffee Date-Walnut Muffins
Soak dates in 10 fl oz strong hot coffee instead of water.

GINGERBREAD MUFFINS

Enjoy this moist tasty muffin in its simplicity or serve warm with extra applesauce and a drizzle of cream for a special treat!

Makes 10-11 standard-size

9 oz (255 g) plain flour*
1½ teaspoons (7.5 ml) baking powder
1 teaspoon (5 ml) bicarbonate of soda
¼ teaspoon (1.2 ml) salt
1½ teaspoons (7.5 ml) ground ginger
1 teaspoon (5 ml) ground cinnamon
¼ teaspoon (1.2 ml) ground nutmeg
1 egg
4-5 oz (110-140 g) light brown soft sugar
2 Tablespoons (30 ml) black treacle or light molasses
   (apply vegetable oil to your spoon to make this easier)
8 fl oz (240 ml) applesauce (ready-made or fresh – see
   note)
2 fl oz (60 ml) milk or water (adjust if necessary)
3 fl oz (90 ml) vegetable oil
3 oz (85 g) raisins (optional)

With self-raising flour, omit baking powder; do not adjust bicarbonate of soda.

Method

1 Prepare muffin tins. Preheat oven to 375-400°F (190-200°C) for a conventional oven, Gas Mark 5-6.
2 In a large bowl, sift together flour, baking powder, bicarbonate of soda, salt and spices.
3 In a separate bowl, beat egg with a fork. Add brown sugar and treacle/molasses, stirring until blended. Add applesauce, milk/water and oil and continue to stir until well mixed.
4 Pour all of wet mixture into dry. Stir just until evenly combined and no dry flour is visible. (Add raisins during the final strokes if using.)
5 Spoon into tins. Bake for 20-25 minutes until tops spring back when pressed lightly.

Note: For fresh applesauce, peel, core and slice 2 medium cooking apples (Bramley or Granny Smith) into a small saucepan. Add a small amount of water – about 3 fl oz (90 ml) water per 8 oz (225 g) apple. Simmer over low heat for 10-15 minutes until the apple is soft and breaking down. Stir apple and water together with a fork allowing small chunks to remain. Cool before using. Measure the specified amount of applesauce for the recipe and sweeten the remainder to serve as a garnish if desired.

LEMON MUFFINS

So simple, so good! Enjoy the delicious variations as well.

Makes 10-11 standard-size

10 oz (280 g) plain flour*
2 teaspoons (10 ml) baking powder
¹/₂ teaspoon (2.5 ml) bicarbonate of soda
¹/₄ teaspoon (1.2 ml) salt
1 egg
3-4 oz (85-110 g) fine white granulated sugar
1 teaspoon (5 ml) finely grated lemon rind (of 1 large lemon) – avoid grating into the white pith which is bitter
1 teaspoon (5 ml) lemon essence (optional)
5 fl oz (150 ml) milk
3 fl oz (90 ml) water
3 fl oz (90 ml) vegetable oil
2 Tablespoons (30 ml) fresh lemon juice

Optional Glaze:
2 oz (60 g) icing sugar, sifted
2 teaspoons (10 ml) fresh lemon juice plus a few extra drops to make a spreadable glaze
¹/₄ teaspoon (1.2 ml) grated lemon rind

*With self-raising flour, omit baking powder; do not omit bicarbonate of soda.

Method

1 Prepare muffin tins. Preheat oven to 375-400°F (190-200°C) for a conventional oven, Gas Mark 5-6.

2 In a large bowl, sift together flour, baking powder, bicarbonate of soda and salt. (Add poppy seeds if using.)

3 In a separate bowl, beat egg with a fork. Add and stir after each addition: sugar, lemon rind, lemon essence, milk, water and oil. Then add lemon juice.

4 Pour all of wet mixture into dry. Stir lightly just until evenly combined. (Add fruit if using.) Batter should have a loose dropping consistency. It will seem thin at first but then starts to thicken. Ignore lumps in the batter.

5 Fill muffin cups three-quarters full. Bake for about 20 minutes until tops are lightly browned and spring back when pressed gently. Stir glaze ingredients together until smooth, pressing out the natural lemon oils from the rind as you stir. Spread immediately over hot muffin tops.

Lemon Berry Muffins
Add 4 oz (110 g) berries, folding gently into the final batter. Chop large berries. Do not thaw frozen berries; bake for an extra 3-4 minutes instead.

Lemon Cheesecake Muffins – with optional fruit topping
Combine 4 oz (110 g) cream cheese with 3 Tablespoons (45 ml) caster sugar. Put a spoonful of muffin batter into 10 muffin cups. Add a spoonful of filling to each and finish with remaining batter. For a special topping, sprinkle a few blueberries on each top before baking.

Lemon Poppy Seed Muffins
Add 1-2 Tablespoons (15-30 ml) poppy seeds.

Lemon Raisin Muffins
Add 3 oz (85 g) raisins or sultanas.

MAPLE PECAN MUFFINS

A Canadian classic . . . and with the goodness of oats!

Makes 10-11 standard-size

1 egg
8 fl oz (240 ml) milk
3 fl oz (90 ml) pure maple syrup
2 oz (60 g) rolled oats
3 oz (85 g) butter or suitable margarine, softened (not melted)
3 oz (85 g) fine white granulated sugar
8 oz (225 g) plain flour*
3 teaspoons (15 ml) baking powder
1/4 teaspoon (1.2 ml) salt
2-3 oz (60-85 g) pecans or walnuts, chopped

Optional Glaze:
1 rounded Tablespoon butter, softened (not melted)
2 oz (60 g) icing sugar, sifted
1 Tablespoon (15 ml) maple syrup (plus a few drops of
    water to thin if needed)

*With self-raising flour, reduce baking powder to 1 teaspoon (5 ml).

Method

1 Prepare muffin tins. Preheat oven to 375-400°F
  (190-200°C) for a conventional oven, Gas Mark 5-6.
2 In a medium-sized bowl, beat egg with a fork. Add milk,
  maple syrup and rolled oats. Set aside to soak while you
  prepare the rest of the ingredients.
3 In a large bowl, blend together soft butter and sugar with a
  spoon.
4 Sift together flour, baking powder and salt. Add to the
  butter mixture and cut in with a pastry blender (or rub
  lightly with fingers) until it resembles fine crumbs.
5 Pour all of wet mixture into dry. Stir just until combined,
  adding nuts during the final strokes. Do not over-stir.
6 Spoon into tins. Bake for about 20 minutes, until tops are
  lightly browned and feel quite firm. Stir glaze ingredients
  together until smooth. Spread thinly on hot muffin tops
  immediately after baking.

MINCEMEAT SULTANA MUFFINS

Loaded with plump juicy sultanas, these are a treat at any time of year!

Makes 11-12 standard-size

10 oz (280 g) plain flour*
2 teaspoons (10 ml) baking powder
1/2 teaspoon (2.5 ml) bicarbonate of soda
1/4 teaspoon (1.2 ml) salt
3 oz (85 g) fine white granulated sugar
1 egg
8 fl oz (240 ml) milk
8 fl oz (240 ml) ready-made mincemeat (about 12 oz/350 g)
3 fl oz (90 ml) vegetable oil
3 oz (85 g) sultanas
Icing sugar for dusting the tops (optional)

Method

1 Prepare muffin tins. Preheat oven to 375-400°F (190-200°C) for a conventional oven, Gas Mark 5-6.
2 In a large bowl, sift together flour, baking powder, bicarbonate of soda, salt and sugar.
3 In a separate bowl, beat egg with a fork. Stir in milk, mincemeat and oil.
4 Pour all of liquid mixture into the dry. Stir just until combined, adding the sultanas during the final strokes. The batter will be lumpy, but no dry flour should be visible. Do not over-stir.
5 Fill muffin cups three-quarters full. Bake for about 20 minutes until tops are lightly browned and spring back when pressed gently. Allow muffins to cool for several minutes to make removal easier. Sieve icing sugar over tops.

*With self-raising flour, omit baking powder; do not adjust bicarbonate of soda.

MARMALADE APRICOT MUFFINS

A warm blend of flavours, this makes an excellent morning muffin.

Makes 12 standard-size

10 oz (280 g) plain flour*
2 teaspoons (10 ml) baking powder
1/2 teaspoon (2.5 ml) bicarbonate of soda
1/4 teaspoon (1.2 ml) salt
1 egg
3-4 oz (85-110 g) fine white granulated sugar
4 fl oz (120 ml) orange marmalade, warmed slightly to improve distribution in the batter
5 oz (140 g) dried apricots, chopped
3 fl oz (90 ml) vegetable oil
1 teaspoon (5 ml) finely grated orange rind – avoid grating into the white pith which is bitter
2 fl oz (60 ml) fresh orange juice
2 fl oz (60 ml) water
2 fl oz (60 ml) milk

Method

1 Prepare muffin tins. Preheat oven to 375-400°F (190-200°C) for a conventional oven, Gas Mark 5-6.
2 In a large bowl, sift together flour, baking powder, bicarbonate of soda and salt.
3 In a separate bowl, beat egg with a fork. Add and stir after each addition: sugar, marmalade, chopped apricots, oil, orange rind, juice, water and milk.
4 When the oven is ready, pour all of liquid mixture into the dry and stir lightly just until evenly combined. The batter should have a good dropping consistency – not too thick, not too thin.
5 Spoon immediately into tins, filling three-quarters full. Bake for about 20 minutes until tops are lightly browned and spring back when pressed gently.

*With self-raising flour, omit baking powder; do not adjust bicarbonate of soda.

OATMEAL CHOCOLATE-CHIP MUFFINS

A popular flavour with a healthy twist. Dried fruit can be substituted for the chocolate chips if you prefer.

Makes 10 standard-size

2 oz (60 g) rolled oats
9 fl oz (260 ml) milk
8 oz (225 g) plain flour*
3 teaspoons (15 ml) baking powder
¼ teaspoon (1.2 ml) salt
3 oz (85 g) plain chocolate chips, either chopped or left whole
1 egg, beaten with a fork
4-5 oz (110-140 g) light brown soft sugar
1 teaspoon (5 ml) vanilla essence
3 fl oz (90 ml) vegetable oil

With self-raising flour, reduce baking powder to 1 teaspoon (5 ml).

Method

1 Prepare muffin tins. Preheat oven to 375-400°F (190-200°C) for a conventional oven, Gas Mark 5-6.
2 In a medium-sized bowl, combine oats and milk. Set aside to soak while you prepare the dry ingredients.
3 In a large bowl, sift together flour, baking powder and salt. Stir in chocolate chips.
4 Now to the milk and oat mixture, add beaten egg, sugar, vanilla and oil. Stir well.
5 Pour all of wet mixture into the dry. Stir just until combined and no dry flour is visible. (Add dried fruit if using). Batter should have a good dropping consistency – not too thick, not too thin.
6 Fill muffin cups three-quarters full. Bake for about 20 minutes, until tops are lightly browned and feel quite firm to touch.

Oatmeal and Dried Fruit Muffins

Replace chocolate chips with 4 oz (110 g) dried fruit such as raisins, dried cranberries or chopped dried apricots.

OATMEAL YOGURT MUFFINS

Just as delicious as they are healthy. Try fresh berries such as cranberries or blueberries for a seasonal touch.

Makes 11 standard-size

7 oz (200 g) plain flour*
2 teaspoons (10 ml) baking powder
$^1/_2$ teaspoon (2.5 ml) bicarbonate of soda
$^1/_4$ teaspoon (1.2 ml) salt
1 egg
4-5 oz (110-140 g) light brown soft sugar
5 fl oz (150 ml) plain yogurt
5 fl oz (150 ml) milk
3 oz (85 g) rolled oats
3 fl oz (90 ml) vegetable oil
3 oz (85 g) raisins or other dried fruit

*With self-raising flour, omit baking powder; do not adjust bicarbonate of soda.

Method

1 Prepare muffin tins. Preheat oven to 375-400°F (190-200°C) for a conventional oven, Gas Mark 5-6.

2 In a large bowl, sift together flour, baking powder, bicarbonate of soda and salt.

3 In a separate bowl, beat egg with a fork. Add sugar, yogurt, milk, oats and oil. Stir well.

4 Scrape all of wet mixture into dry. Stir lightly just until evenly combined. Gently fold in fruit during the final strokes. Batter should have a good dropping consistency.

5 Fill muffin cups three-quarters full. Bake for about 20 minutes until tops are lightly browned and spring back when pressed gently. Frozen fruit may require an extra 3-4 minutes.

Oatmeal Yogurt Berry Muffins
Add 4 oz (110 g) berries. Chop large berries. Do not thaw frozen berries.

ORANGE-CARROT SPICE MUFFINS

The orange-spice combination gives a delicious flavour while the carrot contributes moisture and vitamins. If you prefer to omit the sweet topping, the nuts can be added to the batter instead.

Makes 11-12 standard-size

10 oz (280 g) plain flour*
2 teaspoons (10 ml) baking powder
$^1/_2$ teaspoon (2.5 ml) bicarbonate of soda
$^1/_4$ teaspoon (1.2 ml) salt
$^1/_2$ teaspoon (2.5 ml) ground cinnamon
$^1/_4$ teaspoon (1.2 ml) each ground cloves and nutmeg
1 egg
3-4 oz (85-110 g) fine white granulated sugar
1 teaspoon (5 ml) finely grated orange rind (of 1 large orange)
Juice of the orange plus water to make a total of 6 fl oz (180 ml)
4 oz (110 g) carrot, finely grated (or chopped by food-processor) – yields 6 fl oz (180 ml)
3 fl oz (90 ml) vegetable oil
2-3 oz (60-85 g) raisins, sultanas or currants (optional)

Optional Topping:
3 Tablespoons (45 ml) light brown soft sugar
1 Tablespoon (15 ml) melted butter
2 oz (60 g) pecans or walnuts, chopped

With self-raising flour, omit baking powder; do not omit bicarbonate of soda.

Method

1 Prepare muffin tins. Preheat oven to 375-400°F (190-200°C) for a conventional oven, Gas Mark 5-6.
2 In a large bowl, sift together flour, baking powder, bicarbonate of soda, salt and spices.
3 In a separate bowl, beat egg with a fork. Stir in sugar, grated orange rind, juice plus water, carrot and oil.
4 Pour all of liquid mixture into the dry. Stir just until evenly mixed, adding dried fruit during the final strokes. Batter should have a thick dropping consistency.
5 Spoon into tins. Combine topping, and spoon over tops. Bake for about 20 minutes, until tops spring back when pressed gently.

ORANGE MUFFINS

Delicious fresh orange flavour; use two large juicy oranges, not the tangerine type.

Makes 10-11 standard-size

10 oz (280 g) plain flour*
1¹/₂ teaspoons (7.5 ml) baking powder
¹/₂ teaspoon (2.5 ml) bicarbonate of soda
¹/₄ teaspoon (1.2 ml) salt
1 egg
4 oz (110 g) fine white granulated sugar
2 teaspoons (10 ml) finely grated orange rind – avoid
   grating into the white pith which is bitter
5 fl oz (150 ml) fresh orange juice (2 oranges)
2 fl oz (60 ml) water
2 fl oz (60 ml) plain yogurt
3 fl oz (90 ml) vegetable oil
3 oz (85 g) raisins, sultanas, chopped dates or prunes
   (optional)

Optional Glaze:
2 oz (60 g) icing sugar
2 teaspoons (10 ml) orange juice plus a few extra drops of
   juice or water to make a spreadable glaze
¹/₄ teaspoon (1.2 ml) finely grated orange rind

*With self-raising flour, omit baking powder; do not omit bicarbonate of soda.

Method

1 Prepare muffin tins. Preheat oven to 375-400°F (190-200°C) for a conventional oven, Gas Mark 5-6.
2 In a large bowl, sift together flour, baking powder, bicarbonate of soda and salt. (Add poppy seeds if using.)
3 In a separate bowl, beat egg with a fork. Stir in sugar, grated rind, juice, water, yogurt and oil.
4 When the oven is ready, pour all of wet mixture into the dry. Stir lightly just until evenly combined and no dry flour is visible. Add fruit during the final strokes. Batter should have a good dropping consistency – not too thick or thin.
5 Spoon immediately into tins. Bake for about 20 minutes until tops are lightly browned and spring back when pressed gently. Stir glaze ingredients together until smooth, pressing out the flavourful oils from the rind as you stir. Spread glaze thinly over hot muffin tops.

Orange Poppy Seed Muffins
Omit dried fruit. Add 1-2 Tablespoons (15-30 ml) poppy seeds to the dry ingredients.

PEACH OR RHUBARB MUFFINS

Fresh fruit is ideal for this recipe, but tinned peaches and frozen rhubarb make it possible to enjoy these out of season too. Berries can be substituted here and likewise peaches and rhubarb can be used in the Basic recipe if you prefer a yogurt base (page 12) but don't forget the almond essence.

Makes 12 standard-size

10 oz (280 g) plain flour*
2¹/₂ teaspoons (12.5 ml) baking powder
¹/₂ teaspoon (2.5 ml) bicarbonate of soda
¹/₄ teaspoon (1.2 ml) salt
1 egg
4-5 oz (110-140 g) fine white granulated sugar
¹/₂ teaspoon (2.5 ml) almond essence
5 fl oz (150 ml) cultured sour cream
4 fl oz (120 ml) milk
2 fl oz (60 ml) vegetable oil
5 oz (140 g) peaches or rhubarb, finely chopped (drain well
   if using tinned peaches; do not thaw frozen fruit)
Flaked almonds for topping (optional)

Method

1 Prepare muffin tins. Preheat oven to 375-400°F (190-200°C) for a conventional oven, Gas Mark 5-6.
2 In a large bowl, sift together flour, baking powder, bicarbonate of soda and salt.
3 In a separate bowl, beat egg with a fork. Stir in sugar, almond essence, sour cream, milk and oil.
4 Scrape all of wet mixture into dry. Stir lightly just to combine, folding in fruit with the final strokes. Batter should have a thick dropping consistency as fruit releases juice into the batter as it bakes.
5 Fill muffin cups three-quarters full. Sprinkle with flaked almonds. Bake about 20 minutes until tops are lightly browned and spring back when pressed gently. Frozen fruit will require an extra 3-4 minutes.

With self-raising flour, omit baking powder; do not omit bicarbonate of soda.

ORANGE-DATE BRAN MUFFINS

These muffins, packed with nutrition, were a favourite breakfast and snack food during my childhood. Bran muffins are traditionally served split and buttered.

Makes 12 standard-size

5 oz (140 g) dried dates, chopped
8 oz (225 g) plain flour*
2 teaspoons (10 ml) baking powder
1 teaspoon (5 ml) bicarbonate of soda
¹/₄ teaspoon (1.2 ml) salt
1 egg
5 oz (140 g) light brown soft sugar
1 teaspoon (5 ml) finely grated orange rind
8 fl oz (240 ml) milk
2 oz (60 g) wheat bran
1¹/₂ oz (45 g) wheat germ
3 fl oz (90 ml) vegetable oil
4 Tablespoons (60 ml) fresh orange juice

Method

1 Prepare muffin tins. Preheat oven to 375-400°F (190-200°C) for a conventional oven, Gas Mark 5-6.
2 Chop dates and set aside. In a large bowl, sift together flour, baking powder, bicarbonate of soda and salt.
3 In another bowl, beat egg with a fork. Add sugar and orange rind, stirring till blended. Add milk, bran, wheat germ, oil and dates. Lastly stir in juice.
4 Scrape all of wet mixture into dry. Stir lightly just until evenly combined and no dry flour is visible. Batter should have a good dropping consistency.
5 Spoon into muffin cups. Bake about 20 minutes until tops are lightly browned and feel firm to touch.

With self-raising flour, omit baking powder; do not alter bicarbonate of soda.

PINEAPPLE MUFFINS

Moist and mild with a tasty coconut topping. Buy tinned pineapple in its own juice for convenience. The natural acidity of pineapple reacts with soda bicarbonate to produce a light moist texture.

Makes 11 standard-size

10 oz (280 g) plain flour*
2 teaspoons (10 ml) baking powder
1/2 teaspoon (2.5 ml) bicarbonate of soda
1/4 teaspoon (1.2 ml) salt
1 egg
4 oz (110 g) fine white granulated sugar
3 fl oz (90 ml) vegetable oil
6 fl oz (180 ml) milk
8 slices tinned pineapple, finely chopped – about 8 fl oz (240 ml) when packed in a measuring jug; press out residual juice so the batter will not be too wet
2 fl oz (60 ml) pineapple juice
Desiccated coconut for topping

Method

1 Prepare muffin tins. Preheat oven to 375-400°F (190-200°C) for a conventional oven, Gas Mark 5-6.
2 In a large bowl, sift together flour, baking powder, bicarbonate of soda and salt.
3 In a separate bowl, beat egg with a fork. Stir in sugar, oil, milk, chopped pineapple and juice.
4 Pour all of wet mixture into dry and stir lightly just to combine. Batter should have a thick dropping consistency and no dry flour should be visible.
5 Fill muffin cups three-quarters full. Sprinkle generously with coconut. Bake for about 20 minutes until tops are lightly browned and spring back when pressed gently.

With self-raising flour, omit baking powder; do not omit bicarbonate of soda.

PEAR GINGER MUFFINS

Delicious for snacks – or try them with ice cream or hot custard for a mouth-watering dessert! I like to use tinned pears in unsweetened pear juice for convenience and extra pear flavour.

Makes 11-12 standard-size

10 oz (280 g) plain flour*
2 teaspoons (10 ml) baking powder
1/2 teaspoon (2.5 ml) bicarbonate of soda
1/4 teaspoon (1.2 ml) salt
1 1/2 teaspoons (7.5 ml) ground ginger
1 egg
3-4 oz (85-110 g) fine white granulated sugar
6 fl oz (180 ml) unsweetened pear juice or milk
6 oz (170 g) pear, well-chopped (either tinned or fresh ripe pear)
3 Tablespoons (45 ml) liquid honey
3 fl oz (90 ml) vegetable oil

Method

1 Prepare muffin tins. Preheat oven to 375-400°F (190-200°C) for a conventional oven, Gas Mark 5-6.
2 In a large bowl, sift together flour, baking powder, bicarbonate of soda, salt and ginger.
3 In a separate bowl, beat egg with a fork. Add sugar, juice/milk, chopped pear, honey and oil. Stir well.
4 Pour all of liquid mixture into dry. Stir lightly just until combined. Batter will be lumpy but no dry flour should be visible.
5 Fill muffin cups three-quarters full. Bake for about 20 minutes. Muffins are done when tops are lightly browned and spring back when pressed gently.

With self-raising flour, omit baking powder; do not adjust bicarbonate of soda.

PUMPKIN MUFFINS

In Canada tinned pumpkin is readily available but in Britain I use fresh butternut squash so I can make these year-round. The bright orange flesh is rich in Vitamin A and gives a wonderfully moist texture.

Makes 12 standard-size

9 oz (255 g) plain flour*
2 teaspoons (10 ml) baking powder
1 teaspoon (5 ml) bicarbonate of soda
$1/4$ teaspoon (1.2 ml) salt
2 teaspoons (10 ml) ground cinnamon
$1/2$ teaspoon (2.5 ml) each ground ginger and cloves
1 egg
5-6 oz (140-170 g) fine white granulated sugar
12 fl oz (340 ml) puréed butternut squash or tinned
   pumpkin (see note below)
3 fl oz (90 ml) milk (adjust as necessary)
3 fl oz (90 ml) vegetable oil
2 oz (60 g) chopped walnuts (optional)

Method

1 Prepare muffin tins. Preheat oven to 375-400°F (190-200°C) for a conventional oven, Gas Mark 5-6.
2 In a large bowl, sift together flour, baking powder, bicarbonate of soda, salt and spices.
3 In a separate bowl, beat egg with a fork. Stir in sugar, squash/pumpkin, milk, oil and nuts.
4 Scrape all of liquid mixture into dry. Stir lightly until evenly combined and no dry flour is visible. The batter should have a thick dropping consistency.
5 Spoon into tins. Bake about 20-25 minutes until tops are browned and spring back when pressed gently.

With self-raising flour, omit baking powder; do not adjust bicarbonate of soda.

Note: Cut, peel and cube a butternut squash (at least 500g), removing pulp. Cook in boiling water 20 minutes until soft. Drain, cool completely to let moisture evaporate, then mash and measure. This should produce a thick purée. With tinned pumpkin, increase milk to 5 fl oz (150 ml) as the purée is very thick.

POPPY SEED MUFFINS

Poppy seeds give a unique taste, texture and appearance – they aren't just decoration!

Makes 12 standard-size

10 oz (280 g) plain flour*
$2^{1/2}$ teaspoons (12.5 ml) baking powder
$1/2$ teaspoon (2.5 ml) bicarbonate of soda
$1/4$ teaspoon (1.2 ml) salt
4 Tablespoons (60 ml) poppy seeds
1 egg
3-4 oz (85-110 g) fine white granulated sugar
5 fl oz (150 ml) cultured sour cream
6 fl oz (180 ml) milk
1 teaspoon (5 ml) almond essence
2 fl oz (60 ml) vegetable oil

Method

1 Prepare muffin tins. Preheat oven to 375-400°F (190-200°C) for a conventional oven, Gas Mark 5-6.
2 In a large bowl, sift together flour, baking powder, bicarbonate of soda and salt. Stir in poppy seeds.
3 In a separate bowl, beat egg with a fork. Stir in sugar, sour cream, milk, almond essence and oil.
4 Pour all of liquid mixture into dry. Stir lightly just until evenly combined and no dry flour is visible. Batter should have a good dropping consistency – not too thick, not too thin.
5 Fill muffin cups three-quarters full. Bake for about 20 minutes until tops are lightly browned and spring back when pressed gently.

With self-raising flour, omit baking powder; do not adjust bicarbonate of soda.

SAVOURY CHEESE MUFFINS

A deliciously simple savoury muffin which can be adapted to suit any taste! Some suggestions are given below but you might like to experiment with different kinds of cheese, herbs and other savoury additions. A small amount of sugar is included to improve the texture of the muffin. These are best served fresh and warm.

Makes 10 standard-size

9 oz (255 g) plain flour*
2 teaspoons (10 ml) baking powder
¹/₂ teaspoon (2.5 ml) bicarbonate of soda
¹/₄ teaspoon (1.2 ml) salt
2 oz (60 g) grated cheese (cheddar or other)
1 egg
2 Tablespoons (30 ml) fine white granulated sugar
4 fl oz (120 ml) plain yogurt
6 fl oz (180 ml) milk
3 fl oz (90 ml) vegetable oil
Extra grated cheese or sesame seeds for topping

*With self-raising flour, omit baking powder; do not omit bicarbonate of soda.

Method

1 Prepare muffin tins. These tend to stick to the paper liners more than sweet muffins, so greasing might be preferable. Preheat oven to 375-400°F (190-200°C) for a conventional oven, Gas Mark 5-6.

2 In a large bowl, sift together flour, baking powder, bicarbonate of soda and salt. Stir in grated cheese. (Add dried herbs if using.)

3 In another bowl, beat egg with a fork. Stir in sugar, yogurt, milk and oil. (Add fresh herbs and other chopped ingredients if using.)

4 Scrape all of wet mixture into dry. With a metal spoon, mix ingredients together with a minimum of stirring. The batter will have a thick dropping consistency.

5 Fill muffin cups three-quarters full. Sprinkle tops with extra cheese or sesame seeds if desired. Bake for about 20 minutes until tops are browned and spring back when pressed gently. Cool for several minutes to make removal easier.

Cheese and Herb Muffins
Add 3 Tablespoons (45 ml) chopped fresh basil, chives or other herbs, or about 1 teaspoon (5 ml) dried herbs.

Feta, Red Pepper and Onion Muffins
Omit grated cheese and add the following:
2 oz (60 g) finely chopped feta cheese
3 Tablespoons (45 ml) finely chopped red pepper
4 Tablespoons (60 ml) finely chopped red onion

SUMMER FRUIT MUFFINS

TROPICAL FRUIT MUFFINS

Enjoy these muffins year-round using fresh or frozen berries. Remember to adjust the sugar to suit your taste, taking into consideration the tartness of the berries. (For other berry recipes see pages 12, 20, 36, 44 and 50.)

Makes 11 standard-size

10 oz (280 g) plain flour*
3 teaspoons (15 ml) baking powder
1/4 teaspoon (1.2 ml) salt
1 egg
4-5 oz (110-140 g) fine white granulated sugar
8 fl oz (240 ml) milk
3 oz (85 g) butter, melted or 3 fl oz (90ml) vegetable oil
5 oz (140 g) berries, either alone or in combination, such as blueberries, raspberries, blackberries, strawberries and redcurrants – large berries should be chopped; do not thaw frozen berries

Method

1 Prepare muffin tins. Preheat oven to 375-400°F (190-200°C) for a conventional oven, Gas Mark 5-6.
2 In a large bowl, sift together flour, baking powder and salt.
3 In another bowl, beat egg with a fork. Stir in sugar, milk and melted butter/oil.
4 Pour all of wet mixture into dry and stir lightly just until combined. Batter should have a good dropping consistency – not too thick, not too thin. Gently fold in berries at the end to avoid crushing the fruit.
5 Fill muffin cups three-quarters full. Bake for about 20 minutes until tops are nicely browned and spring back when pressed gently. Frozen fruit will require an extra 3-4 minutes.

*With self-raising flour, reduce baking powder to 1 teaspoon (5 ml).

Moist and fruity, with a deliciously subtle blend of tropical flavours. If you prefer to use juice in the batter, buy tinned pineapple slices in unsweetened pineapple juice.

Makes 11 standard-size

10 oz (280 g) plain flour*
2 teaspoons (10 ml) baking powder
1/2 teaspoon (2.5 ml) bicarbonate of soda
1/4 teaspoon (1.2 ml) salt
1 egg
4 oz (110 g) fine white granulated sugar
4 fl oz (120 ml) well-mashed ripe banana
4 fl oz (120 ml) milk or pineapple juice
4 slices tinned pineapple, finely chopped – about 4 fl oz (120 ml)
4 oz (110 g) dried mango, chopped
3 fl oz (90 ml) vegetable oil
Desiccated coconut for topping

Method

1 Prepare muffin tins. Preheat oven to 375-400°F (190-200°C) for a conventional oven, Gas Mark 5-6.
2 In a large bowl, sift together flour, baking powder, bicarbonate of soda and salt.
3 In a separate bowl, beat egg with a fork. Stir in sugar, banana purée, milk/juice, pineapple, mango and oil.
4 Pour all of wet mixture into dry. Stir lightly until evenly combined. Batter should have a thick dropping consistency.
5 Spoon into tins. Sprinkle generously with coconut. Bake for about 20 minutes until tops are lightly browned and spring back when pressed gently. If your finger leaves an indent, continue baking until done.

*With self-raising flour, omit baking powder; do not alter bicarbonate of soda.

APPENDIX 1

GLUTEN-FREE AND WHEAT-FREE MUFFINS

The terms "gluten-free" and "wheat-free" are often confused. A person diagnosed as "coeliac" is unable to eat any foods containing gluten, including wheat, oats, barley and rye, while someone who is wheat-intolerant might be able to include the other grains in their diet. The recipes in this section are suitable for both gluten-free and wheat-free diets.

There are several gluten-free alternative flours and starches available in health food and speciality shops: brown and white rice flours, maize flour (cornmeal), cornflour (cornstarch), soya flour, chickpea (gram) flour, potato flour (potato starch), tapioca flour and more. None of these flours can produce the same texture as wheat flour. It is the gluten in wheat that gives bread its springiness and other baked goods their desirable texture. On their own, the non-wheat flours produce a dense powdery texture that practically dissolves in the mouth, leaving nothing to chew. Surprisingly, by combining several of these flours, there is a marked improvement which can be enhanced even further by adding extra egg to bind it together.

One additional ingredient produces a dramatic effect: xanthan gum. This is a natural substance, produced by a micro-organism, that has been used commercially in foods (such as salad dressings) for many years. In gluten-free baking, xanthan gum helps to bind the product together to give that special tender chewiness that makes baked goods so pleasurable to eat. If you want to transform your gluten-free baking from substandard to first-class, xanthan gum is the answer! The cost might seem expensive at first but don't let this put you off. As only a small amount is needed, a 100 g tub will go a long way: the price per batch of muffins is minimal.

Xanthan gum is gradually becoming more available for domestic use so you might find it in the special diet section of your supermarket. Alternatively a web search will turn up independent suppliers who stock a wide range of specialist products which you might find useful. Innovative Solutions, for example, stocks a good range of products for gluten-free baking (*www.innovative-solutions.org.uk*).

There are several types of gluten-free flours on the market but they vary greatly in palatability. In the early part of my gluten-free experiments, chickpea flour was quickly eliminated as having an objectionable flavour, at least in a muffin! Soya flour had an unpleasant aroma so that too was avoided. Maize meal (cornmeal), although pleasant, gave the baking a distinctive "cornbread" flavour which did not make it a good base for adding other flavourings.

Product names can also be misleading. British cornflour is a starch and in fact is called cornstarch in North America; it should not be confused with maize flour or cornmeal. Likewise, in Britain potato starch may be labelled potato flour as the two names seem to be used interchangeably. In other countries that might not be the case; potato starch is the required ingredient.

As those on restricted diets are already at risk of nutritional deficiencies, I recommend including some brown rice flour in the following mix, such as 2 oz (60 g) brown rice flour plus 5 oz (140 g) white rice flour. The additional flavour from the brown flour is minimal and quite pleasant. White flour is important for a light texture.

Here, then, is my recommended mix for replacing plain flour, ounce for ounce, in muffins (and many other forms of baking too, but that is beyond the scope of this book!). This quantity makes 10 oz (280 g). Sift the mixture at least twice to distribute the xanthan evenly.

7 oz (200 g) rice flour (ideally a mix of white and brown)
2 oz (60 g) potato flour (potato starch)
1 oz (30 g) tapioca flour (not granules) or cornflour (cornstarch)
1 teaspoon (5 ml) xanthan gum

You can also make up this flour replacement in bulk by increasing each item proportionately. For example, to make a triple batch each item is multiplied by 3, thus 21 oz (600 g) rice flour, 6 oz (180 g) potato flour, 3 oz (90 g) tapioca flour or cornflour, and 3 teaspoons (15 ml) xanthan gum. This should be sifted together several times and stored in a cool, dry place.

Note: When any new food is introduced to a diet, one should be alert to the possibility of adverse reactions, especially in children.

Most of the recipes in this book can be altered to suit gluten-free and wheat-free diets. (Avoid those containing oats and bran.) Remember to increase the liquid slightly, about 2-4 Tablespoons (30-60 ml), and use two eggs instead of one. The batter needs to be quite "sloppy" as rice flour is more absorbent than wheat flour. For best results, choose recipes with a higher moisture content (i.e. with added fruit or vegetables). The two examples which follow demonstrate how to make these adjustments. Enjoy!

GLUTEN-FREE BANANA MUFFINS

Makes 11-12 standard-size

7 oz (200 g) rice flour (ideally a mix of white and brown)
2 oz (60 g) potato flour
1 oz (30 g) tapioca flour or cornflour/cornstarch
1 teaspoon (5 ml) xanthan gum
1 teaspoon (5 ml) gluten-free baking powder
1 teaspoon (5 ml) bicarbonate of soda
$1/4$ teaspoon (1.2 ml) salt
8-10 fl oz (240-290 ml) ripe banana purée (about 3 medium bananas)
4 oz (110 g) fine white granulated sugar
2 eggs, beaten with a fork
3-4 fl oz (90-120 ml) milk or water
3 fl oz (90 ml) vegetable oil
2-3 oz (60-85 g) walnuts or plain chocolate chips (optional)

Method

1 Prepare tins. Preheat oven to 375-400°F (190-200°C) for a conventional oven, Gas Mark 5-6.
2 In a large bowl, sift together at least twice: flours, xanthan gum, baking powder, bicarbonate of soda and salt. (Add chocolate if using.)
3 In another bowl, mash bananas thoroughly with a potato masher. Stir in sugar, eggs, milk/water and oil.
4 Pour all of wet ingredients into dry. Stir until batter is evenly mixed and no dry flour is visible. (Add walnuts if using.)
5 Spoon into tins. Bake for 20-25 minutes, until tops are lightly browned and spring back when pressed gently.

GLUTEN-FREE APPLE SPICE MUFFINS

Makes 10-12 standard-size

7 oz (200 g) rice flour (ideally a mix of white and brown)

2 oz (60 g) potato flour

1 oz (30 g) tapioca flour or cornflour/cornstarch

1 teaspoon (5 ml) xanthan gum

3 teaspoons (15 ml) gluten-free baking powder

1/4 teaspoon (1.2 ml) salt

1 1/2 teaspoons (7.5 ml) mixed spice (adjust to taste)

4 oz (110 g) fine white granulated sugar

2 eggs

6 oz (170 g) finely chopped apple (I like to use Granny Smiths, but most other types should work just as well)

6-7 fl oz (180-210 ml) milk

3 fl oz (90 ml) vegetable oil

2-3 oz (60-85 g) raisins, sultanas or chopped walnuts (optional)

Optional Topping:

3 Tablespoons (45 ml) soft brown sugar

2 oz (60 g) walnuts, chopped

Method

1. Prepare muffin tins. Preheat oven to 375-400°F (190-200°C) for a conventional oven, Gas Mark 5-6.

2. In a large bowl, sift together at least twice: flours, xanthan gum, baking powder, salt, spice and sugar.

3. In another bowl, beat eggs with a fork. Stir in chopped apple, milk, and oil.

4. Pour all of wet mixture into dry. Stir until evenly combined, adding dried fruit/walnuts during the final strokes. This batter is thicker than most; apple releases juice as it cooks.

5. Spoon into tins. Sprinkle with topping. Bake about 20-25 minutes until tops are lightly browned and quite firm.

APPENDIX 2

NORTH AMERICAN MEASURES AND EQUIVALENTS

These are the approximate North American volume equivalents for weights used in this book.
Note: 1 cup = 8 fluid ounces = 240 ml.

Flour

This is only a rough guide as flours can vary considerably. Please read about flour on page 7. When measuring flour by volume, it should be sifted beforehand. It might be necessary to adjust the amount of liquid in a recipe to suit your flour if you are finding the batter too thick or thin. This balance of wet and dry ingredients is important for successful baking.

10 oz (280 g) plain flour = 2¼ cups. *Substitute 1¾ cups all-purpose flour.*

9 oz (255 g) plain flour = 2 cups. *Substitute 1½ cups all-purpose flour.*

8 oz (225 g) plain flour = 1¾ cups. *Substitute 1⅓ cups all-purpose flour.*

7 oz (200 g) plain flour = 1½ cups. *Substitute 1¼ cups all-purpose flour.*

6 oz (170 g) plain flour = 1¼ cups. *Substitute 1 cup all-purpose flour.*

5 oz (140 g) plain flour = 1 cup+2 Tbsp. *Substitute ⅞ cup all-purpose flour.*

Sugar

6 oz (170 g) sugar = ¾ cup
5 oz (140 g) sugar = ⅔ cup
4 oz (110 g) sugar = ½ cup
3 oz (85 g) sugar = ⅓ cup
2 oz (60 g) sugar = ¼ cup

Ingredient	Weight	Volume
Almonds, flaked	2 oz (60 g)	½ cup
Apple, chopped	6 oz (170 g)	¾ cup, packed
Berries	4-5 oz (110-140 g)	¾-1 cup
Bran cereal sticks	3 oz (85 g)	1 cup
Butter/Margarine	2-3 oz (60-85 g)	¼-⅓ cup
Carrot, grated	6 oz (170 g)	1 cup
Cheese, grated	2 oz (60 g)	⅔ cup
Chocolate chips	3 oz (85 g)	½ cup
Cornmeal	6 oz (170 g)	1 cup
Courgette/zucchini	12 oz (340 g)	1¾ cups, grated
Dried fruit	3-6 oz (85-170 g)	½-1 cup
Nuts, chopped	2-3 oz (60-85 g)	½-¾ cup
Oats	2-3 oz (60-85 g)	⅔-1 cup
Wheat bran	2 oz (60 g)	1 cup
Wheat germ	1½ oz (45 g)	¼ cup

Further Notes on Measurement

Although many British units of measurement have the same names as North American (N.A.) units, they are not all identical. In general, weights are equivalent but volumes are not. Here are two differences which may prove useful:

1 British fluid ounce (fl oz) = 28.4 ml
1 N.A. fluid ounce = 29.5 ml

1 British liquid pint = 20 fl oz = 568 ml
1 N.A. liquid pint = 16 fl oz = 472 ml

For single batch muffin-baking, you can assume:
1 fl oz = 30 ml = 2 Tablespoons

To convert fluid ounces to cups, use the following:

2 fl oz = ¼ cup
3 fl oz = ⅓ cup
4 fl oz = ½ cup
5 fl oz = just under ⅔ cup
6 fl oz = ¾ cup
7 fl oz = ¾ cup + 2 Tbsp
8 fl oz = 1 cup
9 fl oz = 1 cup + 2 Tbsp
10 fl oz = 1¼ cups